Always
Keep
Smiling

Wayne

# Much More...
# Laughing & Loving
# with Autism

*A collection of "real life"*
*warm and humorous stories.*

Compiled by R. Wayne Gilpin

Illustrations by Sue Lynn Cotton

**Future Horizons, Inc.
721 W. Abram Street
Arlington, TX 76013**

**800-489-0727     817-277-0727
817-277-2270 fax**

**Website: www.FutureHorizons-autism.com
E-mail:  info@futurehorizons-autism.com**

ISBN # 1-885477-78-3

## Dedication

This book is dedicated to my parents
Douglas and Carolyn Gilpin who, by example,
taught me that the ability to laugh is
almost as important as the ability to love.

# Introduction

Within one's time, there can be a clear seminal moment that improves your life, and, if you're lucky, impact others in a positive way. Such a moment for me was the decision to commit Alex's perspective and humor to a written form, and write "Laughing and Loving with Autism." The original intent was only to be a fun, maybe inspiring, little book. I hoped to enlighten other parents of the joy in our children's different perspectives of the world.

I could have had no idea of the amazing changes the book would make in my life, as well as those of my family and friends. Over 50,000 copies of that book, and its' sequel, "More Laughing and Loving," are out there being read not only by parents, but also by teachers, therapists, and doctors. Even more amazing, this little book led to the creation of Future Horizons, the largest publishing company offering books and videos on autism/Asperger's Syndrome in the world.

From our publishing company, we began offering conferences on autism, Asperger's and related syndromes to parents and professionals all over the world. Candidly, at first the primary intent was to introduce our authors to an audience primarily of parents and a few teachers and other therapists. Our conferences would average 200 to 300 attendees.

Then, the response to the conferences changed dramatically as the interest in autism grew and we changed our marketing approach to focus on professionals as much as family members. Our reasoning was simple. We always want to offer parents a source of assistance for their child. However, for the most part, that parent will work for the betterment of one child, her or his own. A professional, given the right incentives and educational tools, can impact the lives of dozens or even hundreds of children and young adults.

Future Horizons now offers over twenty conferences per year all over the United States and in several foreign countries. We also exhibit at approximately thirty conferences offered by other organizations.

Additionally, I have been honored to ask to speak to audiences ranging from ten to a thousand on various subjects including; the challenges of being a parent, this book, and the humor that helps us to realize the positives in our lives.

There has been an additional benefit that is equally important to me personally: the friends that being involved in autism has brought to my life. There are far too many to mention here individually, but you all know who you are. I thank you for your support, the laughs and the passion you have brought to me. I hope I have given half as much to you as you have to me.

This book is the result, as was the second, of parents, speakers, and professionals offering their stories.

I hope you enjoy the stories and that you will share them with others. However, if they want to borrow your book, politely tell them no, and to go buy their own.

Keep Smiling!
Wayne

# SO-CIALLY FINE

### A Girlfriend for Alex

Recently, Jennifer was speaking to Alex when he casually announced that he had to call a girl after they finished talking. She was pleasantly surprised at this venture into the "social" world. This conversation followed.

"Alex, you're calling a girl? That's great, but why?"

"She is in my social skills class and she gave me her number and asked me to call her. I don't know why."

"Well, what will you talk about?"

"I will just let her talk, it was her idea."

"Well, Alex is she a *girlfriend*?" Jennifer asked with hope surging through her mind.

"Yes, I guess so. She is a girl and she is a friend."

Disappointed but undaunted, Jennifer asked if he would like to have a real *girlfriend*. Alex was unclear as to what she meant, so Jennifer explained that a girlfriend was a person you would go out with on a regular basis and did things with all the time.

Alex said that sounded good and said he would like very much to have a *girlfriend*. Jennifer was feeling that a real special communication with Alex had just transpired, but he burst her bubble when he continued, "How about you, Jennifer; do you have a girlfriend?"

**"That will do it, Ashley, ...or send them packing!!**

Ashley, my 12-year-old daughter with Asperger's, was explaining to our 9-year-old the art of getting a boy to be interested in you. Ashley offered this wisdom to her wide-eyed sibling.

"First, you look away when he stares at you. Then, you blink your eyes at him. But, if you really want him to know that you are serious, you talk about marriage and children."

Kim Hammers
Tyler, Texas

**Way to make friends in the retirement home??**

My grandson visited me in my retirement center shortly after studying American history. We were in the library when one of my neighbors, a lovely elderly lady, was approaching, cane in hand. "Andrew," I said, "the lady there is a friend. Go over and introduce yourself."

He did very well, marching over, putting out his hand and saying, "My name is Andrew Horne, what is yours?" He looked surprised as she said, "My name is Mrs. Madison."

"Oh," he said, "Are you Dolly's sister?"

Bill Hale
Richmond, Virginia

## Sports are great...?

Alex continues to amaze me with his "offbeat" view of life. Recently, he was talking to his sister, Jennifer, who discovered that his roommate was very much into sports. She then asked Alex if he also liked sports. His reply was quick, "Yes, I do!"

As Alex had never shown real interest, she was impressed and a little surprised by this response. So, she then asked him what he liked best.

Alex replied, "Well, I do like sports, except for playing or watching. Everything else I like."

## A "different" way of meeting someone new!

My 9-year-old son with autism, for reasons that were never clear, developed a penchant for bald heads. Any bald head was very interesting to him. However, I didn't know how interesting until one day when we were out at a public function.

I went to get a drink of water for him and me. When I turned around, he was surprising some nice gentleman by standing on a chair behind him and affectionately kissing his bald head. The expression on the man's face was priceless. Thankfully, after some explanation, he was also very understanding.

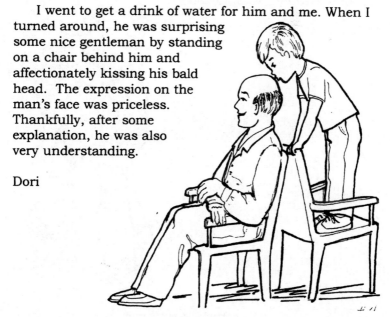

Dori

**Turn Taking**

When my son was about 7 or 8, we were working very hard on teaching the value of turn-taking. He would plunge ahead without thinking of the other child's need to also have a turn at whatever game they were playing. Finally, we thought that we had gotten the message across.

Sometime later, we were at a large family gathering for Thanksgiving. Since it was family, we relaxed and let our son play in the back bedroom with his cousins while we got the rare opportunity to visit with other adults.

We suddenly heard the terrifying sound of a child struggling to catch his breath. Rushing into the room, we arrived just in time to hear our son, who had his arm around his somewhat red-faced cousin's neck, proudly say, "Okay, I'm done choking you. Mother says it is good to take turns. So now it is your turn to choke me!"

Obviously, another lesson in turn-taking was necessary.

Teresa Loftus
Battle Ground, Washington

4

## I think this means I am really loved....

Alex, his sister Jennifer, a friend Polly and I went out to dinner. It was an excellent restaurant in one of the nicest sections of San Diego. Being a fairly upscale French restaurant, we worried that Alex would not find a selection that he would enjoy. However, our fears were put to rest as he spied linguini on the menu. He talked about it constantly before we ordered and after we ordered, but when it arrived he stopped and gave the linguini his absolute attention.

After eating, I went to the restroom. Alex was so absorbed he didn't even see me leave. However, he looked up to find me gone. He turned to his sister and asked where I was.

Jennifer told him and he responded, "That's good, I sure would hate to lose my Dad. I love him very much." This was a fairly rare expression from Alex and both Jennifer and Polly were really touched by the depth of his comment.

However, he followed this sensitive moment by saying, "I love Dad almost as much as, ...as much as, ...THIS LINGUINI!!"

5

**Perceptive—but........to a woman?**

My son Scott is a young adult who is doing very well, living basically independently and of whom I am very proud. I refer to him as a delightful combination of Rainman and Forrest Gump. To prepare this special man for the world, he has had manners drilled into him as much as I think he can possibly stand. Included are admonitions about certain situations that indicate he should be cautious.

One of these was my warning that most adults and particularly woman don't like to discuss their age. However, this training was to little avail when he met a lady and they had this conversation.

Scott—You are a very pretty lady.

Christy—Well, thank you, Scott.

Scott—Do you mind if I ask you how old you are?

Christy—Well, that is a subject that I think we can avoid.

Remembering, (somewhat) my training, Scott recognized that he had ventured on forbidden ground. However, his response to her avoidance was classic Scott.

Scott—Oh, I get it---that means you are really old, huh??

Mrs. Lambeth
Chapel Hill, North Carolina.

**Makes horse sense to me!**

As a young man with Asperger's, I saw the world in a little different light than others. This view led to an interesting exchange with a friend of my mother who, like Mom, was involved in horse breeding. Mother was actually more involved than most and this led to a great deal of discussion about the business around the dinner table. Being highly focused on this field caused me to misunderstand a call from my mother's friend, therefore confusing her with my response.

She called excitedly one day to ask me to relay to my mother that there was a new addition to their family.

I knew Mother would want the particulars, so I asked, "What was the color?" She tried to answer in a way that I could decipher that it was a child, but I was having none of that.

Confused and still trying to get information to relay, I next asked, "Well, do you know who the father is??"

Lars Perner
Washington, D.C

## Grandmother was really flattered

My son Ryan was being invited by his Grandmother
to come to her house to spend the night. It was during a
period when he really didn't like being away from me
and he was resisting. My mother offered this logic,
"Now, Ryan, coming to my house couldn't be the worst
place to go, could it now, dear?"

Ryan pondered the question for a long minute and
then very solemnly said, "No, hell would be worse."

Lisa RA Starnes
Mansfield, Texas


## I love you, Mom, but not yet?

I had Jeremy as an elementary student and then
later in high school. Therefore, I knew his family well
and we enjoyed his company enough to have him over to
our house. One weekend, his folks were going away and
asked if he could stay with us. When they dropped him
off, they said that they would return Sunday at 5:00.

Well, they made better time and arrived at 3:30.
Jeremy was engaged in a game. They went into the
game room and said, "Son, we missed you!"

Barely looking up, he said, "Go away, you aren't
supposed to be here!"

Susan Cataldi
Pittsburgh, Pennsylvania

**Jeremy and his new found hair...or would you like to take him to the barber??.**

My 14-year-old daughter was having a party with her "very proper" friends with everyone trying to be very grownup and adult in their presentations. Suddenly, Jeremy, her brother with autism who was going through the challenges of puberty ventured on the scene. He noticed that one of her male guests had a large amount of hair on his arm. Since he was impressed with the guest's hair, he assumed that the interest would be reciprocated.

Without sufficient warning, he dropped his pants and displayed to the world the four new hairs he had grown, and asked everyone to see!! To my red-faced daughter, this was peer disgrace, humiliation and she was sure that it was the end of her social existence for at least 25 years. However, I would imagine that the attendees will never forget that party!!

Since that day, Jeremy has to be watched closely because he will proudly show off his new "hair" to anyone who mentions the word. As he did with the mailman who had a moustache, the school principal on the first day of school who made the innocent mistake of complimenting Jeremy on his combed hair, or the very surprised UPS lady who was wearing short sleeves with noticeable hair on her arm.

It isn't right for a parent to take some satisfaction in the shock of a nice person innocently caught by Jeremy's tendency to show off his "hair," but if you could have seen their faces......

Sandra Joyce
Harrisburg, Pa.

9

**Leesa's lesson has far reaching impact!**

My youngest daughter Leesa loved to destroy her mother's closet. Leesa is an eleven-year-old girl with autism. She does not understand the concepts of privacy and respecting other people's possessions.

In order to curb this behavior, my wife Karen and I tried many different strategies. We always made Leesa clean up her mess, but after picking up everything in the closet, she would immediately destroy it all over again. Timeouts were useless. We told her in our sternest voices that if she messed Mommy's closet again, we would make Leesa do what she knew were the maximum punishing consequences. We applied one of those punishments each time that Leesa destroyed her mother's closet, but it had absolutely no impact in stopping her.

When it became unbearable, we asked Leesa's teacher Alice Rodriguez how she controlled Leesa's autistic behaviors in the classroom. Alice told us how she used simple signs. Leesa loved to continuously open and close the classroom door. To curb this behavior, Alice showed us the simple picture sign of a door with the international "No" sign taped on it. This sign has been in place and is still working after over six months. To keep Leesa at her desk, Alice taped a simple picture sign of a desk with the wording, "Stay at your chair" on Leesa's desk.

I could not believe that a simple sign could stop Leesa from destroying her mother's closet. Speed limit signs never stop me from speeding along the highways and byways.

Karen and I had nothing to lose, so we taped a sign reading "Don't mess up Mommy's closet" on the closet door. After a few weeks, I asked Karen if the sign was working. To my surprise she answered, "Yes."

10

I couldn't believe it! So I started talking about this experience with my friends at work. One of them, Brad Macmillan, told me how annoyed he was with his teenage son taking and wearing his clothes. Brad told me, "My son takes practically everything I have: pants, jeans, tee shirts, shirts, socks and even my underwear! I have to lock my bedroom door to prevent my son from taking my clothes."

That evening I went to my computer and modified the picture symbol for clothes that Leesa uses with her communication board. It is a simple picture of a pair of pants and a dress with the word "clothes" written on top. I put the international "no" sign over the pant and dress and replaced the word "clothes" with "Don't take Dad's Clothes."

The next morning I gave Brad the sign, and he liked it! He put one on his closet door and one on his dresser. To Brad's surprise and mine, the sign worked immediately. Brad told me, "My son was so stunned by this sign that it took him about ten days to come up with the courage to ask me if he could wear one of my tee shirts."

We shared our success with other staff members. It was the next day that I found that Leesa's lesson would work for more problems than I even dreamed.

That morning when I went into the bathroom at work, I found a sign reading, "PLEASE WIPE THE SINK" with a cartoon character of a maid in the lower left-hand corner. Our office secretary was fed up with the puddles of water that surrounded the sink after people had washed their hands.

I looked down at the sink. The sink and the area around it were spotlessly clean and dry.

Bob Carpenter

### In case you didn't know

My daughter Alison is focused on health and will discuss it any time. However, she will offer well meaning counsel to some who may not appreciate it.

This preoccupation led to an interesting event. One day she accompanied me to a gym. After a workout, we went into the locker room. I didn't notice her wander into the shower area.

There was a very heavy lady finishing her shower, but still lathered with soap and a head full of shampoo. Alison said, "Do you know you're fat?"

Before the shocked lady could respond, Alison added, "But, if you will eat salads or other low-calorie foods and exercise, you will be thinner and have much better health."

Dr. Jeanne McAfee
California

## A note of confidence

My nephew and I were singing together at a family gathering. My energetic but not sophisticated voice was next to his head in our group. After the song, I was impressed with his singing and told him so. "Alex, I wish I could sing as well as you do."

With a slight sigh, he responded, "I sure wish you could sing as well too!!"

Marjorie Langhorne
Livermore, California

## SCHOOL SMARTS

*We parents sometimes have conflicts with teachers, but every parent knows that our children's progress has to depend on caring, sacrificing teachers who, for the most part, do terrific work. This section is about them.*

### Who was that lady?

One of my students, Janice, had a real fondness for a teacher in our building. Every time Miss Lawrence came by, they would exchange pleasantries, often about dogs, a mutual favorite subject.

Well, Miss Lawrence got married and became Mrs. Zelefron. Janice still called her Miss Lawrence. So, I wrote a social story to explain the change. I felt like I had conveyed the concept but I must have missed a step.

Miss Zelefron came in the room and, to my delight, Janice called her the proper name. However, after she left the room, she turned to me and with a puzzled look said, "You know what, Miss Zelefron sure does look like Miss Lawrence!"

Ed Nientimp
Erie, Pennsylvania

## When you don't get the answer from Mother....ask Grandad??

My daughter was the victim of a bully, another girl in her class who teased and taunted her constantly. Constant complaints to teachers and school personnel resulted in no relief from the abuse.

One day as I dropped my daughter off for a visit with my parents, I mentioned this to them, hoping they would have an answer. They seemed concerned, but did not offer any solutions.

About one week later, I received a call from the school to come pick up my daughter because she was being suspended. I was shocked to hear that she had walked into the classroom and without a word had walked up to the offending girl and socked her in the face, knocked her out of her chair, and left her crying on the floor.

I picked her up and took her to my parents' home as I had to go back to work. I didn't want to tell them of her actions but did so reluctantly. When I did, Mother looked shocked, but a strange smile came over Dad's face as he said, "Well, sounds like a good fist to the nose ended that problem." I suddenly realized where the idea for the haymaker had come from.

I do not condone violence, but since that day my daughter has never been bothered by that bully again.

Michelle
Chester, Illinois

16

## Damning with faint praise!

I have a daughter with Asperger's who enjoyed school but did not like a particular substitute teacher. In my attempt to be a good parent, I told her that I would pay her a nickel for every positive thing she could tell me about this particular substitute. She was an ongoing sub, so I felt a need to help her find good things about her.

When Jessica returned home from one school day, I asked her if she was able to find anything positive about this teacher she clearly did not prefer. She looked at me for a long time and then finally spoke, "Well, she left at noon!"

Jolene Thomas
Payette, Idaho

## Ranking of school personnel??

We all know that social language and its nuances are difficult for our children with autism. One day, Chris, a high functioning boy I work with in elementary school showed me how he could master the art of a put-down, at least in his mind.

He had just beaten me in a language game we were playing. In mock humiliation, I said, "Chris, you have no idea how embarrassing this is for me. Here I am, a teacher, and I have just been beaten by a student."

With an expression of mock scorn, he said, "You're not a teacher now. You are just a substitute school bus driver!" He then fell off his chair laughing. In his view of the world, I had the ultimate humiliation.

Tim Draper, SLP
Chehalis, Washington

## Good perspective!

Matt, a young boy with Asperger's is one of the members of the basketball team that I coach. However, I have learned that my "pep talks" do not always impact him as they do the other players and clearly not the way I intended. He was always concerned about our winning, tried his best and seemed bothered when we lost, which I must admit was almost all the time.

We were going into a game and I said to the group, "This is your team, this is your game to win or lose." I noticed from Matt's expression that this seemed to make a real impression. I felt pretty proud of making this breakthrough. Well, the game was pretty close and I could see that he was following the game pretty intensely. I realized how intense he was when he left the bench to walk out on the floor and, to my shock, give the signal for time-out.

I asked him what he was doing. He replied, "You said it was my team and I decided we needed a time out!" I told him that the team was my responsibility and I would decide when time outs were necessary.

Well, we lost that game by a larger score than usual. However, Matt was very casual and did not seem to be bothered at all. When my wife asked the reason for his new attitude, he said, "See Mr. Gray. He's responsible for us losing!"

Brian Gray
Jenison, Michigan

## Let's Face It

Finding one of her students making faces at others on the playground, Ms. Smith stopped to gently talk to the child.

Smiling sweetly, the schoolteacher said, "Bobby, when I was a child I was told that if I made ugly faces, it would freeze and I would stay like that."

Bobby looked up and replied, "Well, Ms. Smith, you can't say you weren't warned."

Autism Advocacy Magazine


## Not That Tasty

My son, Ryan, was struggling with his math. I said, using the logic that had been given to me as a child, "Ryan, you can do it. Math is a piece of cake." He looked up very excitedly as he asked, "Cake, great. Where is it?"

When I explained that there actually was no cake and what I said was just an expression, he lost interest in my explanation and went back to his homework. After working for a while, he looked up to me with sad eyes and shook his head as he said, "Mom, math is definitely not a piece of cake, it is a piece of spinach!"

Allison Woods
Sugarland, Texas


## Ask the right question!!

Mrs. Rainwater wanted my son John to help her pass out water bottles at school. She asked him to count heads to see how many there were. He looked around the room intently and then turned with a very puzzled expression and responded....
"Everybody has just one!"

Linda Contellanos
Rome, Georgia

# PARENTS CAN SAY THE DUMBEST THINGS!!!

*Those who know me well are aware that I am a big proponent of parent/heroes taking an active role in their child's life. I support them demanding the best services available. This activity will naturally take them to the often-dreaded IEP meeting. I believe they should be assertive, but positive, in their service requests. However, sometimes they go too far. These comments were made by well meaning parents at IEPs or worse, public events.*

Temple Grandin was taking questions at the end of a presentation. A lady put her hand up and asked, "My son likes playing with cars, how does autism cause that??" For the longest thirty seconds of that woman's life, Temple just stared at her and then looking away, said, "Next question."

■ ■ ■

A parent was in her son's IEP and asked, "My son seems to resent it when I hit him, is that because he has autism?"

■ ■ ■

Another Mother asked, "He doesn't like spinach. Will he like it if I call it something else?"

■ ■ ■

Another very optimistic parent was requesting ABA training specializing offered by Dr. Ivar Lovaas of the University of California at Los Angeles. The program called for 40 hours a week of intensive one-on-one training, all to be paid by the school for an estimated cost of $25,000. Before the school personnel could even respond, she added, "I **know** you will do the Lovaas method, but who will pay for Dr. Lovaas' housing while he is in town for the school year?"

■ ■ ■

A parent stood up when I was speaking and asked me if Alex had ever said curse words. When I replied, "no," she said, "Well, if you want to hear some really good cursing, just come over to my house after the presentation." I was unclear as to why she thought I needed that interesting experience.

■ ■ ■

Two parents argued all through the IEP. Finally, the father stood up and said, "This is your problem, I'm damn sure that no genes from my side of the family had anything to do with this kid's autism!" The room was silent after the Father left as the professionals were embarrassed for her and had no idea what to say.

Finally, the Mother broke the silence, and the pressure, saying, with a slight smile, "He doesn't know it, but his genes had nothing to do with this kid at all!"

## TEACHERS AND SCHOOL OFFICIALS CAN ALSO SAY "DUMB THINGS"

Vice-Principal—Your son has the cutest red hair and freckles. I just love the time we spend together. I've really come to know your situation very well.

Parent—My son doesn't have red hair or freckles.

Vice-Principal—(looking puzzled) Are you sure??

■ ■ ■

Another professional, the school psychologist, said, "My years of training and experience in the field assures me that your son has all the characteristics of austisism." When everyone stared in disbelief, he said, "What's wrong, haven't you heard of austisism?"

■ ■ ■

The school principal stuck his head in the door during a very fractious IEP and wisely offered, "Let me see now, this meeting *is supposed* to be about helping Jason with **his** social skills, right??"

■ ■ ■

A special education director, after hearing that the child was having sleep problems, turned to the gentleman seated next to the Mother and asked if he let the child into bed with he and Mrs. Wallace. Without blinking an eye, the *new* school psychologist said, "I doubt that my wife, Mrs. Jones, would appreciate it if either the child or Mrs. Wallace got into bed with me."

■ ■ ■

Then there was the classroom teacher who explained how deeply concerned she was at being able to handle a child with autism in her class the next year, and then fell asleep halfway through the IEP meeting...and snored.

●●●

The IEP team leader who upon meeting the parent for the first time said, "The report says that Pat has been going to the girl's bathroom often during the day. Why do you think he is doing that?" The Mother patiently said, "It may be because Pat is a girl."

●●●

A school psychologist offered this monument to edu-babble—

"It is the professional judgment of this examiner that J-------'s lack of ability to function in an independent manner is having a detrimental impact on his functioning independently!"

## HOW TO TELL A REAL TEACHER!!

Real Teachers...

- Grade papers in the car, during commercials, in faculty meetings, in the bathroom and, when under pressure at the end of a grading period, during church.

- Cannot walk past a line of kids without straightening up the line.

- Are written up in the Guinness Book of Records for the elasticity of their kidneys and bladders.

- Can tell you after one week of a new term which parents will show up at Open House.

- Cheer when they hear that April 1 does not fall on a school day.

- Have never heard an original excuse.

- Buy Excedrin and Advil at Sam's.

- Will eat anything that is put into the teacher's lounge.

- Have disjointed necks from writing on the blackboard while watching the class.

- Know that secretaries and custodians run the school.

- Hear the heartbeat of crisis, always have time to listen, and know they teach students, not a class.

## ODE TO A TEACHER

Teachers who care about our kids are special in many ways.  This poem, written by a parent, illustrates how parents feel.

Special Teacher

You held the key that unlocked
The chains of silence
You planted a seed that was nurtured
By the grace of your caring.

These are the doings of the heart
They are not read about or formulated
Although the skill was learned from the
Backbone of text
You have left the harsh lines behind
Solid in technique.

You held out your hand
It was open, safe and easy to grasp
Your hand opened a door to a new and exciting
World waiting to be explored
You shined a light that caressed the seed
That blossomed into my son.

The world awaits this curious boy
Who was shown the key to grow
You've done your work well
The fruits of your labor are evident in the
Sparkling eye, the smile and the touch of my boy.

You have done your job well
The seed you tenderly nurtured has taken root
And will now grow, prosper and be full of joy.

Greg Buckingham
Fletcher, North Carolina

### Elvis lives!

In choosing Alex's senior year courses, we were down to picking one more course. With some caution, I chose drama. Alex was willing to go along, but wasn't even sure what they did in a drama class.

(To other parents, this was one of the best judgments I made about Alex's education. He responded well and grew because of the experience.)

One day, Alex came home from school with an assignment that struck fear in my heart. Students were to each choose a famous person and act like them in front of the class so the rest of the class could identify the star. Alex chose Elvis Presley. Now, in singing you have two challenges. First, to remember the words and the second is to sing well. Let's just say that Alex remembers words very, very well.

So, I was worried that his lack of the second skill (I'm afraid he inherited his father's voice) would be embarrassing. So, I told him that prior to his presentation, scheduled in three days, we would choose a different person.

The next day I picked Alex up at school. His drama teacher happened to come by and casually mentioned that Alex had done his performance that day as a couple of kids were out of class, and they moved Alex up. My heart was sinking as I asked how he did.

The drama teacher said, "Great! The whole class screamed out, 'Elvis!' after Alex walked up to the mike in the front of the room, shook his arms and body slightly and said, in a deep voice, 'Thank you. Thank you very much.' "

And, they say our kids can't be creative.

# GOTTA LOVE 'EM

**Uncles are always an easy touch!!**

My brother Tommy was visiting with my daughter who has autism. She was trying to reach over the microwave to get some candy purposefully put there to keep it out of her reach. Tommy watched her efforts waiting to see how she would try to solve the problem.

Suddenly, she got a look over her face as obviously an idea had come to her. With a small smile, she got a cardboard box and placed it in front of the cabinet. fearing the box would collapse, my brother started to stop her. However, he stopped short when he realized that she had placed it with the open top up.

With a look of expectation, she stepped into the open box, only to find that her reach had not increased. She then wisely turned to her best hope, Uncle Tommy, and raising her outstretched arms to him, simply said, "please!"

The tactic worked. Her uncle could not resist those beautiful eyes.

Hollie Pierce
Euless, Texas

# Careful with your everyday witticisms

My son Dustin went through a period of not eating well. After some encouragement, he began eating better and we took him back to the doctor to see how he was improving. However, since the last visit, he had a new collection that he treasured.

Well, the nurse put him up on the scale and was impressed with his weight gain. She said, "Wow, you have gained a lot of weight. Terrific! It's almost as if you had rocks in your pockets."

You guessed it. His new collection was rocks which he had proudly stowed away for safekeeping and now pulled out to show her. The stunned nurse was flabbergasted that, for once, someone did, in fact, have rocks in their pocket. Without a word, she just brought him back to the waiting room and left. I'll bet she never asked that question again.

Dale Lucht
Molalla,
Oregon

26

**Alex is full of compliments.**

I have this disconcerting habit, to others, of turning my blinker on before I actually have to. (No, it is not an age thing! I've done this since I was a teenager.) My daughter Jennifer hates it and brings it up whenever she can. We were driving in California and I, by error, not only hit the turn signal before a turn was coming, but it was actually a turn in the road, not a turn off the road. We all laughed and Jennifer said, "He did that, because he's my Dad!"

Alex, from the back seat, calmly said, "No, Jennifer, he did that because he's dumb."

**A gentle smile!!**

Sometimes people with autism will do the most touching things.

When my brother was a little kid, he would let an adult know that he liked them by backing up to them, take their hand and put it gently over his shoulder and just hold it for about 20 seconds.

Jennifer Gilpin
Los Angeles, California.

**Adults say the dumbest things**....

A mother of one of my students was in the grocery store. After finishing her shopping, she got into a line that turned out to have a customer who could not find her check book, identification or anything else to finish the purchase. Obviously, this caused a long wait.

To no one in particular, the mother said, "I always get into the wrong line."

Her daughter, looking up at her with a confused look, said, "Why do you do that, Mom?"

Carol Gray
Jenison, Michigan

**One man's view of an emergency is not the same as another's!!**

We worked with our son to be able to meet unusual circumstances in his life, including an in depth lesson on dialing 911 if there was an emergency. We spent time explaining how to call, information he should give, etc.

Well, one day he was alone downstairs involved in his favorite activity of watching movies playing on the VCR. He loves his videos so much that he has them memorized and catalogued in his mind. We had a problem with movies that we rented because he did not want to return them. He would hide them from us. We always find them but only after long searches. Sometimes he would even go to the point of tearing off the labels so we could not identify them as rented. For his purposes only, he remembered these by the barcode on the side.

This fateful day, we heard a scream from our son who pointed out that the VCR was not functioning. I jumped into the problem and after a few minutes had it running again. He had left the room but arrived back looking very relieved.

My wife passed by the phone and noticed that it was off the hook. She picked up to find a very frustrated 911 operator telling her not to worry because rescue personnel were on their way to handle the emergency that had just been called in.

You guessed it. To us, it was a VCR temporarily not working, but to him it was as dire an emergency as he had ever experienced and a call to 911 was certainly called for.

Bill Davis
Lancaster, Pa.

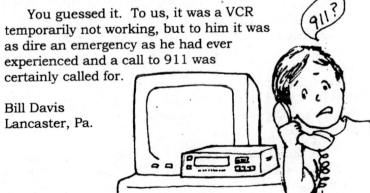

## More thirsty or thirsty for more

His father sends a small boy to bed. Five minutes later:

"Da-ad..."

**"What?"**

"I'm thirsty. Can you bring me a drink of water?"

"No. You had your chance. Lights out."

Five minutes later: "Da-aaad...? I'm THIRSTY. Can I have a drink of water??"

"I told you NO! If you ask again, I'll have to spank you!!"

Five minutes later... "Daaaa-aaaad..."

"WHAT??!!"

"When you come in to spank me, can you bring me a drink of water?"

Autism Advocacy Magazine

## A different view!

The little girl walked by the aquarium at the super market. It was loaded with lobsters, catfish and other fish swimming around unaware of their fate.

She stared for a little while, and then with a gentle smile, turned to her father and said, "Look, Dad, they have pets!"

## A "touching" face...

It was a very hectic morning for both my son Alaeric and myself as we tried to get ready to leave for kindergarden. He was acting resistant to getting his shirt buttoned and kept turning away.

I'm sure with more frustration in my voice than I planned, I said, "Turn around here and face me!"

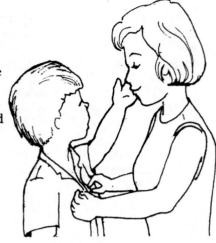

Alaeric looked surprised and confused for just a second, then he turned around and began tenderly stroking my face. This moment defined my role in his life.

Tami McQueen
Anchorage, Alaska

## Come on, Dad, what are you thinking?

My eight-year-old AS son Alex and I went away for a weeklong visit to my brother's home. When we returned home, my husband took a look at our very tall son and said, "I could swear that you grew another foot!"

You guessed it. Alex looked down with a puzzled look on his face as he tried to comprehend such a stupid comment, and said, "No, I still have only two."

Mr. Pope
Towson, Maryland

## Accurate descriptions

Sometimes my son with autism describes things much more accurately than we mere mortals who do not see things as clearly. One time he looked up at the half-moon and said sadly, "Look; the moon is cracked!"

Another time after his sister lost her two front teeth, he said, not as sadly, I will admit, "Sarah's smile is really broken!"

Sally Mustard
Urbana, Illinois

## Andy wouldn't mind

I work with a 34-year-old man who loves music, especially the songs of Andy Williams, Glen Campbell and Johnny Mathis. In fact, in the morning he has breakfast with them...well sort of. He lines up their albums around the breakfast table and tells them of his upcoming day.

A new staff member asked him he had ever met Andy Williams. He responded that he had seen him in concert and had actually met him. The staffer was impressed and asked him how he felt meeting such a big star. He was immediately corrected as he was told that Andy Williams was not a big star at all.

All within hearing distance were shocked to hear this coming from such a big fan...until he continued by saying, "He is not big at all. He is just a little, short guy... much smaller than I am."

Debbie Wilson
Decatur, Illinois

## A strange exchange

Mother was in the bedroom replacing the diaper on her youngest while her son with autism played alone in the other room. The doorbell rang. From a third room, Dad called out, "Sweetheart, can you get that?"

Mother replied, "I can't; I have to change the baby."

The son, somewhat anxiously, yelled out, "What's wrong with the one we have?"

Becky Moyes
Pittsburgh, Pa.

## In other words...

Whenever Alex's sister went out for a drive, I always said, "Turn on your lights and lock the doors." One day Alex said, "Why do you always say that, Dad?"

I was a bit taken aback but, after consideration, offered what I thought was an answer that would satisfy the question. I said, "It is really my way of saying, I love and care for you."

He looked pensive as he played with his fingers as he always does when concentrating, then looked up and said, "Why don't you just tell her that you love her and care for her?"

The logic of that comment so overcame me that I had no reply. However, three weeks later I was throwing on my jacket, adjusting my tie, and rushing out of the house late as usual for an appointment.

Alex, looking at the floor, but aiming his voice at me, said, "Dad, turn on your lights and lock your doors."

# RELIGIOUS REFLECTIONS

## "What do you say to that, Father?"

I run a camp for young adults. One of them, whom we will call Bob, had a problem with ordering things at the food line or anywhere else where he had to ask for service. So we practiced, and he seemed to be getting better. However, I didn't know how much better until I, at his mother's request, took him to a Mass being held close to the camp.

He decided to take communion and I thought it best to go with him, although I am not Catholic. We were at the altar as the priest came up with the wafer. Before he could offer it, Bob said, in a voice you could hear in the back of the church, "I'll have one body of Christ, please!"

Dr. James Ball
New Jersey

## It might work

An exasperated mother, whose son was always getting into mischief, finally asked him, "How do you expect to get into Heaven?"

The boy thought it over and said, "Well, I'll just run in and out and in and out and keep slamming the door until St. Peter says, "For Heaven's sake, Jimmy, come in or stay out?"

Autism Advocacy Magazine

## Nice way to meet the new minister

Our son James was going to have his tonsils out. Our new minister kindly and dutifully came to the hospital to give support. After some opening conversation of encouragement to James, we had a general conversation covering several subjects. Somehow, the subject of drinking and driving came up and the dangers associated to children. We were all very seriously discussing this important matter, when James suddenly interrupted with this "conversation stopper." "Dad, you drink and drive all the time!"

I looked in shock from James to the minister to see how he was reacting to this "second party" confession. He looked as surprised as I did, and I noticed that he was no longer looking my way. Abashedly, I asked James when I had done so. With typical honesty, he said, "Just this morning, you drank a Pepsi as we drove to the hospital!"

I was glad to see the smile on the minister's face as he realized that to James literal world, "drinking was drinking."

John Guyest
McConnellsburg, Pa.


## No bird-brain

In order to make a point to the children assembled around him during the Sunday morning service, our Rector used a parable. To make it dramatic, he told of a little bird that caught in a snowstorm.

Suddenly, my heart stopped as my son Ben raised his hand. Every eye in the church turned to my son as he said, "I'm sorry, Father, but birds would not be in a snowstorm, they fly south for the winter."

The congregation roared with laughter as the somewhat red-faced Father Henry sheepishly said, "You're right, Ben." Somewhat took the drama out of the story.

Laura Schroeder
Flower Mound, TX.

**Take this question---and tell me I'm not thinking.**

I was working with a student with autism, who defied the notion that those with this challenge cannot think in the abstract. We were having an electric storm, and he seemed deep in thought.

Then he turned to me, and asked, "When lightning flashes, does God have to change the light bulb?"

Leone R. Ham
Montana

**Good perception**!!

At a church service for handicapped people, Mother and Neil were sitting in front of a handicapped child who made a distressing high pitched bleating sound every time there was a lull in the proceedings. That led to this conversation.

Neil: Mother, there's a lamb in the church.

Mother: Huh??

Neil: I didn't know they allowed sheep in the church.

Mother: Shut up!

Neil: Maybe it is the lamb of God,

Helen Benson
Upson, England

## Of course he was a saint

We are practicing Roman Catholics. My son Gregory, diagnosed with Asperger's, is 13 years old and an altar server at Mass. He was very close to my father who passed away at 83 when Gregory was 11. I realized how much he loved him when he said to me shortly after my father died, "I think Pop-Pop should be named a Saint (canonized)."

We home-school Greg in religious education so I patiently pointed out to him that it was a lengthy process, including three documented miracles.

His response was, "Well, he certainly must be a saint because he was the kindest man I ever knew."

Maureen Norcie

## No quite what I meant

Getting up early was never easy for Alex. One morning I remarked that he looked like a zombie.

"What's a zombie?" he asked.

I tried to put my response in a way that someone who had never seen a horror movie might understand. "Alex, it is when a person dies, is buried, and rises from the grave to walk among the living with their hands held out like this," I said as I held my arms out.

Incredulously he asked, "Jesus was a zombie?"

## WORD FUN & GAMES

### Doggone good thinking!

We were explaining to our Asperger's student that some people "overeat." He looked confused by this concept, but brightened up when he added, "Well, all dogs overeat."

It took the therapist a few moments to understand that the student thought overeating meant eating *over* a bowl or plate.

Sue Ellen Spangler
Garland, Texas

### Logic?

My son communicates through typing and sometimes tries to get my attention quickly when he can't get to the typewriter. On one such occasion, he grabbed my arm and scratched me. Trying to guess his need, I asked him if he needed an aspirin. He shook his head in the affirmative.

To try to gain from the moment, I said, "Since you can type, you could type that to me that you have a headache and need an aspirin. You do not have to scratch me!"

His logic in reply was a bit confounding, "Well, next time, I bet you'll ask me first!"

Betty Thompson
Richmond, VA.

**Mother, can't you see my face?**

When my son Xander was five years old he ate, by himself, a big jelly toast. As he joyfully ate it, some of it actually got into his mouth, the majority going everywhere else.

"Xander, what is this all over your face?" I demanded.

"Cheeks!" He accurately answered to a question that to him was probably silly.

I washed him off laughing, knowing that this kid was going give me lessons in asking questions in the years to come.

Carla Humbert
Chico, Ca.

**That's catchy!**

Alex goes monthly to a meeting of ARC adults, who are *"a group of self-advocates,"* according to the ARC, called UP WITH PEOPLE. That name, it had been discovered, was already copyrighted for the use of another group of young people. So the group of self advocates had to change its name. The ARC then asked each member of the group of self advocates to suggest a name that he or she thinks might be a good new name.

Alex told me that his upcoming suggestion, which he said he thought was really good, was going to be...
"A GROUP OF SELF ADVOCATES."

## Can they teach us "unique" profanity?

Xander was alone in the living room when my husband Mike and I heard a loud crash. We ran in to find the desk tipped over and papers everywhere.

What happened?? Mike asked, even though at the time Xander had very little language.

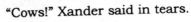

"Cows!" Xander said in tears.

We looked at each other, forgetting all anger and just trying not to laugh.

To this day, when we have no idea what "cows' meant. However, it was one of his first words and he has used it often when angry, distressed or trying to get out of a demand. He uses it as a profanity, basically.

Then one day, I was surprised to hear my husband, after banging his finger, yell out "Oh, cows!" It is now a family expression. We all yell, "cows" when life is not going our way.

Carla Humbert
Chico, Ca.

## Entirely too much time at K-Mart!

We were sitting down for our Thanksgiving dinner, and I said that we should each say a little prayer about our family. Each member said something appropriate and I finished with "All of us are for one and one for all!"

My son picked up on this and said, "Yes, one for all.... and today, we have a special of three for five!!"

Marianna Bond
Fort Worth

41

## What would Mr. Fudd have to say?

My son is developing a sense of humor, although a little offbeat. He was at the dinner table when his younger sister asked if rabbits could talk. Without missing a beat, Jared, who we didn't even know was listening, said, "Sure they do. They say, 'What's up, Doc?'"

When I looked at him, very surprised, I noticed a very big grin on his face.

• • •

His use of words is unique, if not always clear to us mortals. One day, he asked me if I would have stripes like Grandmother when I got that old. It took me a while to realize that he was referring to wrinkles. I told him that Grandmother earned her "stripes," and I was certainly earning mine.

• • •

He has developed a terrific ability to recognize states and countries by their shape. One day, while we were fighting the good fight of toilet training, he excitedly called me to come into the bathroom.

Fearing the worst, envisioning all kinds of disasters, I rushed in to find him pointing excitedly in the toilet and saying, "Look Mom, Madagascar!!"

Ester Friesen
Meade, Kansas

42

## Honestly...

I was driving my sons Lance and Troy to school one morning and stopped at a red light to chat with a friend who sells papers there. He puts a paper in the car for me and we drove away.

"Mom, you didn't pay. Did he give you that for free?" asked Troy.

"Yes, I have friends in high places, Troy." I joked.

But Lance piped up, "You mean like in Canada and Alaska?"

Diane Murrell
Houston, Texas

## So that is where it went!

My son Adam has a very healthy appetite but is still thin. One day, after a particularly robust meal, I told him he ate like he had a hollow leg. He agreed.

Later than night, as he prepared for his bath, I noticed his tummy sticking out because of his posture. I asked him if his tummy was full from eating.

He said, "No, but my leg is sure packed!"

Denise Komraus
Monaca, Pennsylvania

# WORKING

## Happy Birthday...when?

Having a person with autism in your workplace has many positives, and I often tell people that. Mike has had a genuine impact on our office in many ways. One is that he has changed our ritual of having birthday parties.

One year it came time for his party and I told him to come into the conference room as we were going to sing Happy Birthday to him. To my shock he refused. When I asked him why, he replied that we could not because his birthday was actually the previous Saturday and this was Monday. He was adamant.

So, I thought for a little bit and asked him if it was okay if we sang "Happy Birthday, last Saturday." He smiled and said that would be just fine.

Thereafter, whenever anyone is having a birthday on a weekend we always add in the appropriate day. It was really fun when one person had their birthday while on vacation and we had to sing, "Happy Birthday, Tuesday before last."

**Mike tries to keep Annette informed.**

One of our co-workers has autism and has somewhat latched onto me to be his guide at work. One day he came in and accurately described why he was late for work, "my buzz-buzz clock did not buzz-buzz."

He also overheard a few of us talking about beer and seemed to want to be in on the conversation, something he rarely does. So, I asked him what kind of a beer man he was and he replied, "I am a ice water type beer man."

Mike also hates bugs and brought my attention to a problem in his area by drawing in great detail, how the rug and lamp would look with bugs on it. He even had creases in the rug. When asked what they were, he said he had to put those in because bugs could be hiding in there.

He also came to work and asked me to look in his hair because he had passed under a tree and asked me to examine his head to see if a twig, branch, or limb had fallen in his hair.

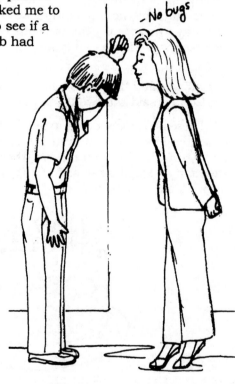

Annette Vick
Arlington, Texas

46

## Off to work??

My nine-year-old son Andrew enjoyed putting on a suit and tie to "go to work."  I was delighted by this pretend play and would encourage it by saying, "Have a great day!" and other things you say to a person going off to work.

One September day, he changed into a navy blazer and tie.  He put on his bike helmet and went out to ride his bike on the pavement right in front of our house.  When, after being distracted by the phone, I did not see him, I went out looking for him.  To my shock, no Andrew!

I immediately called the police and within an amazingly few minutes, there were hundreds of police, volunteers and a helicopter combing the neighborhood.

This went on for the longest four hours of my life.  Then the phone rang, it was the police telling me that he had been found in downtown Baltimore.  He had traveled miles and through some dangerous neighborhoods and busy streets.  To this day, I have no idea how he did it.

The police escorted this relieved but still distraught mother to the Central police station.  There were many police officers standing around waiting to see this frantic parent reunited with her son, who they thought would be just as happy to see me as I was to get him in my arms.

As I held out my hands to him, he brushed right past me, and in typical autistic fashion said, "Ride bike....Go to work."  The officers were shocked, both at his words and at my seeming not to be bothered with the smile still on my face.

Paige Pope
Towson, Maryland

47

## Salesman of the Year???

I was quite proud of Alex when he worked with me at the ASA conference in San Diego. I taught him how to sell the conference proceedings manual. He had learned the important factors of the book very well and related it to everyone who came near the table. He handled money, credit card machines, helped with inventory, etc.

A woman showed up at the table, exclusively to speak to Alex. She was endearing as she said, "Alex, I saw you at the ASA conference in North Carolina when you sang "You'll Never Walk Alone" at the closing of the conference. It was one of the most dramatic moments of my life and I had tears of joy in my eyes for an hour after you spoke. I just wanted to meet you and tell you what that meant to me."

Alex looked at her and without missing a beat said, "So, do you want to buy a book?"

## Future Horizon's #1 employee!

There is a delightful young man with autism who works in our office. He is a treasure because things like stuffing envelopes that everyone else hates, he enjoys and does the task faster than anyone. Recently, he worked a few more hours than usual, and I gave him a little bonus also. This caused him to write the following letter to "yours truly."

*Dear Wayne, (It took about four years for him to call me Wayne, I was always just the Boss.)*

*Thanks so very much for when the last time I was paid. I was paid One hundred and fifty dollars and sixty-six cents. Yes. $150.66. That made me feel really happy because that was so much more of a good amount of money for me to be paid for.*

*Your most loyal and favorite employee,*
*Mike*

## Alternative send-off

Recently when I was leaving a company for another opportunity, I was going around giving hugs to most of the office staff. However, when I came to a co-worker who has autism, I reached out my hand. He looked at me and said, "I'm sorry, but I cannot touch your hand because you have been eating a bagel. But, I can do this."

With that he stood up from his chair, and walked around behind me and patted me on the back like a child.

Jennifer Gilpin
North Hollywood,
California

49

## SENSORY FUN

### Do you hear what I hear?

My son David loves bathrooms and visits them as soon as possible wherever we go out. On a visit to Grandmother's, he came out of the bathroom looking very disappointed. We asked what was the problem. He responded, "Why doesn't your sink talk to me?"

Having no idea what he was talking about, we followed him into the bathroom for an explanation. He ran some water and then held his ear into the sink to listen as the water ran quietly out. "See, it doesn't talk to me," he said very disappointingly.

We were confused until he made a gurgling sound. That's when we realized that this was the sound made by our bathroom sink at home. David heard that sound entirely differently, and more sensitively, than anyone else!

Diana Stadden
Tacoma, Washington

**Can you see what I see?**

About three months before this book was published, I took Alex on a vacation to Zion National Park in Utah. Unless you have been there and can draw on that memory, I can't think of words to describe the beauty of the canyon. I really wanted Alex to share that feeling. I was constantly pointing out vistas and he nodded, but clearly I was not getting the reaction I thought the beauty deserved.

Finally, we turned a corner to a truly breathtaking view as we entered a large canyon with the cliffs changing color as they rose to the sky. I said, "Alex, look up; what do you see?"

He looked up, turned to me and the other tourists who were listening, and said with boredom hanging on each word, "More rocks."

✦✦✦

Alex recently spoke before an audience of over 500 on a panel of high functioning people with autism. The other panel members were Caroline Smith and Steven Page. Steven, the most high functioning of the group, was in the middle. Because I was the moderator, I was standing on their side and could see down the line of the panelists.

While Steven was speaking, Alex and Caroline were stimming with alternate rocking motions during his entire presentation. First, Caroline would rock forward and then Alex, in almost perfect timing. I was worried that poor Steven would get sea-sick.

To his credit, he never missed a beat and finished his entire presentation without even noticing their rocking.

✦✦✦

*One of our favorite people is Jerry Newport from Los Angeles. Himself a person with Asperger's Syndrome, Jerry is the founder of a group called AQUA, a joining together of adults with Asperger's Syndrome or High Functioning Autism. Jerry is known for his kindness and gentle, sensitive view of the world. However, he is equally recognized for his wit and sense of humor.*

Recently, with tongue firmly stuck in cheek, Jerry came up with a diagnosis list of ways you can tell if you are a teenager or adult with Asperger's. Enjoy!

**You could have Asperger's if more than half of these apply to you:**

1. *You think Al Gore moves and talks normally.*

2. *As a child, rather than riding a bike, you turned it upside down and moved the pedals to watch the wheels move.*

3. *Your think "Spin City" is a show about autism.*

4. *As a kid you played with a hamster by putting him on a record turntable.*

5. *Your favorite movie of all time is "Groundhog Day."*

6. *You think Judge Judy should "chill" and just let everyone talk.*

7. *You believe that the action on the World Wrestling Federation is real.*

8. *You see nothing funny in the "Who's on First" routine.*

9. *You could sing several stanzas of "Louie-Louie" in church and not understand why that is not proper.*

10. *You would prefer a parrot to the speech therapist*

11. *Your favorite kitchen utensil is the egg beater.*

12. *You think Bill Gates is "too cool."*

13. *You hate "Simon Says" and always lose.*

## The wisdom of Temple

Anyone who has attended a Future Horizons conference knows that Dr. Temple Grandin is one of our favorite people. She is special not only for her caring for people with autism/Aspergers, but also for the unique perspective that she brings to the world. At one of our recent conferences, one of the attendees very gently asked Temple if she feels she missed out by not going to the senior prom, college parties, etc. that are so much a part of many lives.

Temple seemed bemused by the question and replied with perfect Temple logic, "No, I don't. In fact, I feel sorry for all of you who wasted your time going to all that silly stuff. While you were doing that, I was studying and learning. Think what you all could have accomplished if you were doing what I was doing! This would be a pretty sad world if all the people who accomplish important things were spending all of their time at parties!"

## ANOTHER VIEW OF ALEX—FROM HIS MOTHER!

Alex and I were watching a TV special on Frank Sinatra three weeks after the crooner's death. I was curious as to how he would like this style of music from this late, great entertainer.

"Alex, I bet seeing these old film clips of this man makes you think he is a real old-fashioned guy."

"It sure does. I also think he is a real old-fashioned dead guy!"

✦✦✦

Alex sometimes can be a challenge to one's ego. I had called and left word on his answering machine, but he had not replied. When I reached him, I was slightly bothered and asked why he had not called.

His answer stunned me, "Oh, was that you? I thought the voice sounded familiar!"

So much for 20 years of raising a child!

✦✦✦

Alex was preparing for a trip to California obviously with some apprehension he had not mentioned before. I said, "Alex, this invitation is for a nice TEACCH dinner when you get back from your trip. It's something to look forward to."

Very calmly he answered, "Well, that is if I don't get killed in an earthquake."

✦✦✦

My husband Nat was listening to the radio, and Alex asked which station he was listening to that evening. I replied (not realizing that I was heading for a "pun-trap!) that it was 1360 am.

Again the grin came over his face, and he replied, "It's nighttime. Why is that a.m. station on the air?"

✦✦✦

Hoping to help Alex with his Christmas shopping, I suggested that he buy a Neil Diamond tape for my husband and me.

He answered, "Ah, Mom, well, I'd really rather spend my money on myself."

✦✦✦

Alex often shows a depth of understanding that belies his challenge. He loves to create puns. Recently, I was talking to him about his passion to do things on time and very exactly.

He gave me that grin and said, "Mother, that is because I have precise-ism!"

✦✦✦

I told Alex that we had an appointment at the social security administration. He asked what it was for. I told him it was to get government benefits for him. He didn't know what that meant.

After a long pause, he asked, "You're not going to put me in the army, are you?"

Starla Clement
Chapel Hill, North Carolina

## *Alex in Cyberspace*

**As a gift, and with some apprehension as to how well it would be used, Alex received a computer with e-mail capacity. To the delight of his mother and I, he began using it and rapidly grew into the great communicator of the 21st century. However, Alex's "unique" perspective in verbal language made us smile and laugh when his words came through cyberspace.** *(Editor's note: We did not change Alex's grammar or spelling so you could get the full flavor of his words.)*

### E-mails...with love, from Alex

*This is to his sister (he really does know her first name!). Note in this and virtually all other e-mails that Alex loves food and also assumes that the person he's e-mailing to isn't all that bright.*

Dear Gilpin

Actually Jennifer as I told you on the phone I am not going to camp after all. I do hope to see you this Friday.

It was Saturday when I went to see the show called One. That same night we went to A Restaurant called Umberto's, it was A very nice Italian restaurant, and for dinner there I had the Shrimp Scampi it was very good. Another night while we were at Myrtle Beach we ate at another nice restaurant called the Parson's Table I like it too for dinner there I had the Fillet Mignon it was A kind of steak which they take A piece of bacon and wrap it around the steak itself it was really good.

Love Alex

Dear Dad

Thank you for these interesting thoughts. I really enjoyed them. I really liked the one that said "A day without sunshine is like eh...night." I especially like that one. I sure had a fun time with you at Thanksgiving. I really liked the show called the *Granbury Live*. I actually liked the scene in that show where this girl tells Santa or whatever his name was that she wanted elves for Christmas and he thought she said she wanted Elvis for Christmas.

Once again I want to thank you for these interesting thoughts. I hope to be hearing from you soon. Take good care of yourself. Goodbye.

Love Alex Gilpin

Dear Dad

Thank you for the Top Country songs of the Day. I enjoyed reading them. As I told my Aunt Carole I do like Country music but I don't like to listen to it. I also want to thank you for the warning about when my M&M's Jukebox thing will come.

I hope we will have a good time in Baltimore this Christmas. I think you (and all of my aunts and uncles) are my number one reason I want to come to Baltimore. Because I wanted to see these people. I hope to be hearing from you soon. Take good care of yourself. Goodbye.

Love Alex Gilpin


Dear Jennifer Gilpin,

So Jennifer you went to see a movie called *Amelie* huh. You said that it was a good movie do you think I would like it? Well let me tell you while I was in Texas seeing my dad we went to two movies. One was called the *Black Knight* and the other one was the *Harry Potter* movie. Have you heard of the *Harry Potter* movie before? Well as I just told you the *Harry Potter* movie was the other movie I saw with my dad. I know that if you ask him, he'll tell you that that's the truth. I hope you have had great Thanksgiving. I want to hear all about it.

Did you have lots of Turkey, Ham, and/or Mashed Potato's and Gravy. Well I sure did. I had Turkey, Ham, Mashed Potato's and Gravy, and a Green Bean Casserole and it was all so good. I hope to hear from you soon. Take good care of yourself. Goodbye.

Love Alex Gilpin


Dear Aunt Carole

I sure am glad your leg is healing. It would be bad news if it was getting worse. Aunt Carole when I told you that I had Chicken Fingers at the K&W Cafeteria I didn't mean that the chicken had fingers. I just meant that what I ate were like strips of fried chicken. Tonight (12/3/01) Scott and I had another Social Skills thing with TEACCH and we were in two different groups (Yes Scott was in one group and I was in another one).

Guess what, when I went bowling with my group on one of my turns I got a strike (You know it's what you get when you knock down all the pins in one roll of your bowling ball).

Love Alex Gilpin


Dear Ms Colleen Gilpin

That's great that you are going to California to visit my sister Jennifer and then to Hawaii. Now Ms Colleen Gilpin I want to hear about your trip when you come back home okay. My roommate Scott and A friend of ours named Shelley And I went to see the Disney movie called the "Princess Diaries" and I thought it was funny. I liked the two parts where the actors were playing baseball and the batter hits the ball and the ball hits other people. If you don't understand why I would think that was funny you might want to see the movie.

I hope you have A great time in California and Hawaii. Again I want to hear about your trip. Take care now. Goodbye.

Love Alex Gilpin


Dear Jennifer Gilpin

I just read the E-mail about donating Campbell's Soup and I liked it. Thank you so much for it. Your right it would be a good idea to donate any kind of food especially to the people who are hungry and have no food.

I hope you are having a wonderful day. Take care now. Goodbye.

Love Alex Gilpin

*Interesting view Alex has of one of the outstanding autism programs in the world.*

Dear Aunt Carole

I am so glad that you liked the part of my last E-mail where I had told you that I told two of the stories from my dad's book *Laughing and Loving with Autism* to the people who were at the TEACCH dinner and sitting at my table. TEACCH is a program held by Dr. Gary Mesibov and it has something to do with autism.

Goodbye.
Love Alex Gilpin


Dear Jennifer Gilpin

Yes we will be seeing each other at Jeff's wedding. It does sound like you had a lot of fun at Melanie's birthday party playing "Planet Hollywood" and playing "Outburst" and doing all the other things you had mentioned. Tell me when you were playing "Planet Hollywood" did you get any of the questions about movies or T.V. right? Also when you played "Outburst" did you guess any of the words on the word list? I sure hope you did.

Let me tell you on Sunday night Scott and his community partner Diedre (Pronounced DEE-dra) and I went out for dinner at a restaurant called Sal's Pizzaria Ristorante (The last word in the name is pronounced REE-stor-ON-tey). At this restaurant I ate the Fettucini Alfredo with Shrimp on top. It was so good. Then on Monday night I went with a small group of members from TEACCH and we all went to a cafeteria in the University Mall called the K&W. There I ate the Country Style Steak with Mashed Potatoes and Gravy and Creamed Corn on the side. Take care now. Goodbye.

Love Alex Gilpin

Dear Aunt Carole

So Pumpkin Pie is your favorite huh.  In that case you must really like that kind of pie.  I am so exited that Don will be getting a job at the Dollar General Store.  I would like to hear all about what he does at his new job.  So if you wouldn't mind telling me all about it I would appreciate it.  Tonight Scott, and a couple of friends named Todd and Cristina, ate at a restaurant called Bailey's Pub and Grill.  Did you know that the word Pub means bar?   Well it does.   Anyway there at the restaurant we all shared some Quesadillas. (Pronounced CASE-a-DEE-a's) as an appetizer.  For my dinner though I ate a Bacon Cheeseburger with some French Fries.  It was so good I loved it.  I hope to hear from you soon.  Take care now.  Goodbye.

Love Alex Gilpin


Dear Aunt Carol

Yes I'd love to send you my mother's E-mail address.  Now Aunt Carol if you have A bad memory on E-mail addresses and if you have A printer you should print this E-mail out. Anyway here it is, it's swclement@... There now you have it.  Also in case you don't have my dad's E-mail address here it is it's dashgilpin@.... There now you have my dad's E-mail address.

Take care now.  Goodbye for now.

Love Alex

P.S.  In case you saw that in this E-mails subject I put Starla Clement instead of Starla Gilpin and your wondering why it's because she is now married to A man named Nat Clement and she now got the same last name as Nat.

*The following was in response to my writing to Alex telling him that he did not have to respond to joke emails.*

Dear Dad

   Dad, the reason I replied to the E-mails about jokes and other interesting things is because I wanted to thank the person who sent me that interesting E-mail. In other words I thought it would be kind of rude for me to just not say anything at all.   I didn't want to do anything that makes the people sending me those E-mails feel like they're not being a good enough E-mail sender.  I just wanted to do what I can to make them feel good.  I hope you understand that.  I am glad to hear that the conference went well and that they LOVED the story about the linguini.  I hope to hear from you soon. Take good care of yourself.  Goodbye.

Love Alex Gilpin


*Alex was invited to his cousin's wedding and wrote about it, especially the food, with a surprise reference to yours truly.*

Dear Aunt Carole

   Let me tell you about Jeff's wedding.   His wedding went great.  To add to this wedding update the wedding was held at the Congrational Club in Washington D.C. We had a great time at his wedding.   We ate Fried Chicken and Salmon for dinner at the reception.  It was really good food.  Their also was dancing and music at the reception too.  But most of all I liked being with my dad.  So I was glad that he was there.  I think he is the nicest dad to be around.  But Again we had a fun time at Jeff's wedding.   I actually wish you could have been there at his wedding.  I will be hearing from you soon. Take good care of yourself.  Goodbye.

Love Alex Gilpin

*Neat e-mail that shows his sense of humor. It also shows his lack of respect for segues.*

Dear Aunt Carole

Aunt Carole I know you think that I am a funny guy but I can't help it because I have a disease called "Saying Funny Thingstism". It is a disease that makes me a funny guy. Yes I also have made my mother laugh before. So your birthday is on January the 25th huh.

I hope neither you nor Uncle Larry let the dogs out again or else one of you might have to sing that song WHO LET THE DOGS OUT WOOF WOOF WOOF WOOF I will be hearing from you soon.

Take good care of yourself. Goodbye.

Love, Alex Gilpin

Dear Aunt Carole

So you have a State Fair in Oklahoma huh. Well if you say you liked it you must have been to the State Fair. Is this True? I was sending Jennifer's mother Ms. Colleen Gilpin an E-mail telling her about us going to the fair and she sent me an E-mail back saying that she hadn't been to an amusement park in a long time and that she had forgotten how much fun it was and that my E-mail that I sent her reminded her of that. Did you see what I told you about what Scott and I did for lunch today in my last E-mail I sent you? Well if you didn't I will repeat it. Today Scott and I went to the K&W Cafeteria for lunch and I ate the Grilled Chopped Steak, Mashed Potatoes and Gravy, and Creamed Corn.

To answer your question about what movie we watched we watched *Toy Story 2* (the sequel to the movie *Toy Story*) I liked it very much although I liked the first one *Toy Story* better because in both movies Buzz Lightyear uses the line TO INFINITY AND BEYOND! Not that I think that is a bad line it's just that since I never heard that line until I saw the first movie *Toy Story* I thought that the first one was more original. I hope to hear from you soon. Take good care of yourself. Goodbye.

Love Alex Gilpin


Dear Aunt Carole

I think we should do everything we can to protect this country from having any future terrorist attacks once and for all. Yes that is right because I (just like every body else) like our country very much. So I think we should let everybody live as long as possible. Again I think we should prevent any future terrorist attacks like the one that recently happened at the "World Trade Center" and the Pentagon in Washington D.C.

If it is possible I would like you to print this E-mail out and share it with all the people you love very much in our remembering of the day these terrorist attacks happened. Yes the people I want you to share this E-mail with includes people in your family. This will show them how much I care about our country. I hope you agree with what I think about our country. What I said about keeping this country is what I think should happen to it especially for the people we love. Remember United we Stand and God Bless America. Take care now. Goodbye.

Love Alex Gilpin

P.S. Even though I am only 22 I would appreciate it if you would take what I said about this country seriously.

*A discerning reader will find that the North Carolina basketball team did not have a very good year.*

Dear Aunt Carole

I am glad you will let everyone know how I feel about our country. Let me tell you what we (Scott and I) did this weekend. Saturday 9/22/01 we went to a football game. it was the North Carolina Tarheels playing against the Florida State Seminoles. Surprisingly our team (North Carolina Tarheels) won and not only that, we won by a lot of points. I said surprisingly we won because the other team Florida State Seminoles is usually a very good team and usually wins.

Take care now. Goodbye.

Love Alex Gilpin



Dear Aunt Carole

Aunt Carole yes I thought it was very sad that our team the North Carolina Tarheels lost on Thursday night. My roommate Scott really likes sports but I don't (okay at least not the way Scott likes them). As I told my sister Jennifer one time I do like sports but I don't like to watch them or play them. Do you like sports? If so what is your favorite sport?

Let me tell you what Scott and I did today (Saturday 11/3/01). Today Scott and I went with Scott's community partner Diedre (Pronounced DEE-dra) to a carnival at the dorm where Diedre stayed when she went to college at U.N.C. (The University of North Carolina) called the Fall Carnival. At this carnival they had lots of food and games. The food I ate at this carnival was pretty good I ate some cupcakes and pretzels and candy corn and chips. I played two of the games there. One was Bingo (you know that game where they call out these numbers and if you get 5 in a row you call out

Bingo) if you get Bingo you get a prize. Well guess what I did get a prize playing Bingo. The prize I got was a pumpkin with candy in it.

The other game I played was one called the Cake Walk (No we did not walk on a cake that is just what they called the game). The way this game is played is you have to walk on these numbers in a circle while the music is playing. Then when the music stops you stand on the number nearest to where you are.

I hope you are having a great day. Take good care of yourself. Goodbye.

Love Alex Gilpin


Dear Aunt Carole

I actually do like violent movies. I just don't like to watch them. Yes I have heard some new Rock and Roll songs like Enya singing "Only Time". At least I think that is what the name of the song is. Unfortunately, I forgot how this song goes. I certainly liked it when these trick or treaters came to your door and they said TRICK or TREAT to you and you gave them there candy then asked them where is the trick. Well Aunt Carole I don't think they mean there is a trick. I think it is just a saying kids use. I think you ought to know that by now.

I did go to a Pizza party (yes I did have pizza two nights in a row) and to watch the Georgia Tech vs. the North Carolina Tarheels game. Sadly our team (the North Carolina Tarheels) lost. I hope you are having a great day. Take good care of yourself. Goodbye.

Love Alex Gilpin

### Alex's touching email to his sister Jennifer

Dear Jennifer Gilpin

Jennifer Gilpin, I am sorry I didn't get to see you at Christmas in Baltimore. I heard you had to go back to California. I am not positive but I think it's because you had some plans for Christmas there. I sure do wish you could have been in Baltimore to see me for Christmas though because I really like you a lot. I was worried that you did not know that!

I hope to hear from you soon. Take good care of yourself. Goodbye.

Love Alex Gilpin


Dear Jennifer Gilpin

Jennifer I am so sorry that when you ordered you pizza and your Dr Pepper and your salad that the waiter forgot your salad. That must have been a disappointment especially if you like salads.

I went to a dinner where I told the people some of the stories from Dad's book "Laughing and Loving with Autism" like the one where the boy named Chris was in church and shouted "TOUCH DOWN". Do you know which one I am talking about? I also told them the one where Chris Purdue went to the wrong class and told the teacher that he has been here before and that the teacher has just not seen him because sometimes he's "invisible". They loved it. I hope you are having a great day. I'll be hearing from you soon. Take good care of yourself. Goodbye.

Love Alex Gilpin

Dear Aunt Carole

Aunt Carole thank you for the E-mail called "What Am I?" That was so nice for you to think of me. I really liked that E-mail. Wow, you made 260 cookies! Well, you sure did make a lot of cookies. I sure hope Leslie (or whatever her name is) wasn't to upset when you told her not to eat the cookie dough.

Last night (12/10/01) Scott and I went with a friend of ours named Shelley to see the new Walt Disney movie called *Monsters Inc.* I really liked it. It's a movie about these monsters that go around and scare kids and also go around the world or something like that. I like the fact that one of the way's they go around the world is by going through these doors and they are already in another part of the world. I really liked that movie.

Did you see any good movies lately? If so I want to hear about them and what their names are. I hope you are doing fine and that your leg will be getting better. I hope to hear from you soon. Take care of yourself. Goodbye.

Love Alex Gilpin


Dear Aunt Carole

I am sorry I didn't sign my last E-mail "Love Alex" at the bottom. I accidentally pushed the send button. Anyway as I was saying I don't know what we will be doing this weekend. I don't even know when the next time Scott and I will go bowling will be. Also I would like to make a correction.

The song by Styx is called "Come SAIL Away With Me" not Come Fly Away With Me like you said. For information on what Scott and I did on Monday night and Tuesday night please refer to the last E-mail I ended up not signing "Love Alex Gilpin" at the bottom.

Love Alex Gilpin

Dear Mom

Mom I know that you said that was a nice E-mail I sent you but did you get the part about me telling you what Scott and I did on Saturday? I hope you did. Also I am excited that we are going to the Neil Diamond concert on 3/12/02. Hopefully nothing bad will happen just like the last Neil Diamond concert you tried to go to but ended up not going because of what happened to your sister Mary.

Also I know you asked about the basketball game. So let me tell you about it. It was the North Carolina Tar Heels playing against the Maryland Terrapins. The final score was 92-77. Sadly our team (The North Carolina Tar Heels) lost. That's the bad news about our team they just aren't doing so well this year. I hope to hear from you soon. Take good care of yourself. Goodbye.

Love Alex Gilpin


Dear Aunt Carole

No I didn't enjoy those Peanut Butter Cups that you gave me I just liked eating them Plus the ones that my mom gave me I didn't like them either I just liked eating them. Except that the ones that my mom gave me are a little bit bigger but that didn't stop me from enjoying them. I enjoyed them as much as I enjoyed the Peanut Butter Cups you gave me. Plus my grandmother Mati gave me some cookies and things like that (It was sent to me a little bit late but that's okay).

Let me tell you what Scott and I did over the weekend. On Saturday February 16, 2002 Scott and I went to a baseball game. It was the North Carolina Tar Heels (Yes the North Carolina Tar Heels do have a baseball team as well as a basketball team and a football team) playing against the Seton Hall (Pronounced SEE-ton Hall) Pirates. The final score was 4-2 with this baseball game going into an extra inning.    Sadly our team (The North Carolina Tar Heels) lost.    Then on Saturday night Scott and I went to the K&W Cafeteria for dinner.    There I ate the Honey Glazed Chicken, Mashed Potato's and Gravy, and Creamed Corn.    Plus I had a Pepsi to drink.    Now Aunt Carole, I don't think I have Honey Glazed Chicken before so this was a new thing for me but I liked the Honey Glazed Chicken.

Then on Sunday Scott and I went out with a friend of ours named Megan to the bagel shop called Bruegger's Bagel Bakery.    Plus Scott and I are now learning how to use a bus system. We are doing this so that in the future if there is something that Scott and I want to do and nobody is able to do it with us and we are going to a place that the regular bus system can't serve we will be able to do it.    Anyway at Brueggers Bagel Bakery I ate a ham and cheese and Honey Mustard on a new kind of bagel that I don't think I have had before. This kind of bagel is called the Asiago Parmesian (Prounounced OS-ee-O-go Parmesian).    Plus I ate some chips along with this bagel.    They including the bagel were all really good.

Then on Sunday afternoon Scott and I went with a friend of ours named Todd to a basketball game.    It was the North Carolina Tar Heels playing against the Florida State Seminoles.    The final score was 95-85 and guess what the North Carolina Tar Heels won.    GO TAR HEELS.    So that's what Scott and I did over the weekend.    I miss you very much and hope to hear from you soon. Take good care of yourself. Goodbye.

Love Alex Gilpin

Dear Jennifer Gilpin

Thank you for wishing me a Happy Valentines Day. I want to wish you a Happy Valentines day too. I hope you had a great Valentines Day. I sure did. I didn't do anything special though. Did you get any Valentines Day Candy? Well I sure got some Valentines Day Candy from my mother. This Valentines Day Candy is some Reese's Peanut Butter Cups with little Hearts on top and they were really good.

Just the other night I got an E-mail from my Aunt Carole telling me that she and Uncle Larry are going on a trip to Grand Field, Oklahoma and that while they are on this trip they are going to go to a drug store. You might never believe this but guess what the name of this drug store is (Hint think of my last name). If you said it is called the Gilpin's Drug Store you guessed it. That's right it is called the Gilpin's Drug Store. What do you think of that a Drug Store with my last name. Wouldn't you be shocked if there was a place with the same as name as your name? Think about it. I again hope you had a nice Valentines Day. Take good care of yourself. Goodbye

Love Alex Gilpin


Dear Jennifer Gilpin

I am sorry you didn't get any Valentines Day candy. Maybe Valentine's Day isn't popular in the area where you live.

Jennifer I would like to make a correction the name of the DRUG STORE that Aunt Carole is going to is the Gilpin's Drug Store it's not the name of the town like you said (At least I think that's what my Aunt Carole told me).

I didn't share any of my Valentines Day Reese's Peanut Butter cups although my roommate Scott did get some Reese's Cups too. He thought they were really good. Yes I really love my grandmother Mati very much and I thought that was very nice for her to think of me. I miss you very much and hope to hear from you soon. Take good care of yourself. Goodbye.

Love Alex Gilpin


Dear Jennifer Gilpin

Jennifer, it does sound like you had a lot of fun at this conference in Monterrey, California, and on this boat ride where you got to see the seals.

Let me tell you what Scott and I did this weekend. On Friday, Scott and I stayed home and watched the American Music Awards. They had singers like Alicia Key's, Janet Jackson (You know, Michael Jackson's sister) getting awards. The singer Aaliyah (Pronounced ah-lee-yah) got an award, too, although I heard she was killed in a plane crash which I thought was kind of sad because I really liked her.

Then on Saturday Scott and I went with Jayson and Heather to the Tar Heels basketball game against the Virginia Cavaliers. The final score was 71-67. Sadly, our team lost. But the good news about this is that we were at least in the game.

Sunday Scott and I went into the music store where I bought a CD of a band called the Zombies. Have you ever heard of them? They are an old band; in fact, I think they are one of those from the 50s or 60s. They sing songs like *Tell Her No* and *Time of the Season*.

So that's what Scott and I did over the weekend. I hope to hear from you soon. Take good care of yourself. Goodbye.

Love Alex Gilpin

Dear Jennifer Gilpin

Yes, I did like the sweat shirt or whatever it was you gave me. Thank you for this shirt? By the way, did you get my email about what I did in Seattle, Washington, and in Baltimore, Maryland? If so, what did you think of it?

Let me tell you what Scott and I did today. Today, Scott and I went with a friend of ours named Todd to a basketball game. It was the North Carolina Tar Heels playing against the Wake Forest Demon Deacons. The final score was 84-62 and sadly our team (The North Carolina Tar Heels) lost. Scott and I sure would have been a lot happier if our team won. Although I heard that the Wake Forest Demon Deacons has a good basketball team. So I kind of thought we might lose. Again though, we weren't happy when we knew that our team (The North Carolina Tar Heels) lost. I hope to be hearing from you soon. Take good care of yourself. Goodbye.

Love Alex Gilpin


Dear Dad

Dad I have two things to tell you. First of all I want to thank you for forwarding that E-mail called Hmmm????---More food for thought! to me. I really liked it. I hope you will send more E-mails like this one because I like it a lot. Secondly I just want to remind you that my birthday is coming up. In fact it is this coming Wednesday when my birthday will be. Take good care of yourself. Goodbye.

Love Alex Gilpin

*In a way the following may be the best email Alex sent. He loves coming to the Future Horizons conferences, meeting the people, enjoying the other speakers (not to mention the good food). I offered to bring him to our conference in Maine, casually mentioning that, for this conference, we did not have room for his roommate, Scott, who we often invite.*

*At first read, I was disappointed because Alex would not be coming. Then I realized the implication of Alex sacrificing for a friend.*

Dear Dad

I am feeling fine. I would rather not go to the conference in Portland, Maine, because of the fact that Scott will not be able to speak at that conference. I would like to come but not without Scott. He would feel bad.

I hope you have a great day and to be hearing from you soon. Take good care of yourself. Goodbye.

Love Alex Gilpin


Dear Jennifer Gilpin

So you went to Boise, San Francisco, Ontario for work at conferences huh? Well I would like to know if these conferences were on autism. If so did my dad speak at any of these conferences? And if so did he tell the people at these conferences any of the funny stories about me? If so which ones do you know he told? Also when you do think of the name of that italian restaurant you celebrated your birthday Please tell me the name of it. I hope to hear from you soon. Take good care of yourself. Goodbye.

Love Alex Gilpin

Dear Ms. Colleen Gilpin

Thank you for the 21 Guidelines that you sent me I really enjoyed them. I especially agree with suggestion #15 Say bless you when you hear someone sneeze. I always do that when my roommate Scott sneezes. Just for your information Scott sneezes really loud when he sneezes.

Let me tell you what Scott and I did this weekend. On Saturday Scott and a friend of ours named Todd and a friend of his named Chad and I went to a football game. It was the North Carolina Tarheels playing against the E.C.U. Pirates (East Carolina Pirates). The score was 24-21 and guess what our team (the North Carolina Tarheels) won. GO TARHEELS! However chad went to college at E.C.U. (East Carolina University). Since that was the case he pulled for the E.C.U. So he was a little sad that his team lost.

Then on Sunday we went with Kelly, who works for a company called R.S.I. (Residential Services Incorporated) to an event called Pig Pickin. This event is like a Barbecue. They had lots of food. There at this event I ate some Pork Barbecue and some Beans and Spegetti. For dessert I ate some Pumpkin Pie. I hope you had a good weekend just like I did. I'll be hearing from you soon. Take good care of yourself. Goodbye.

Your friend Alex Gilpin

### *Is this a "subtle" hint for more?*

Dear Mom

Thank you for that nice shirt from Wyoming that you gave me. It was so nice for you to think of me. I think that I will wear this shirt soon that is how much I like the shirt. I sure hope you can give me more presents like this one in the future. I really would like it if you would do that. Once again thank you for the shirt.

Love Alex

Dear Ms Colleen

Thank you for the Irish Bracelet Message. That was
very nice for you to think of me. You must be thinking of
me A lot because you have been sending me A lot of E-
mails. That must mean that you really like me as A
friend (which I hope you do). I really like you A lot it's
more than the fact that you send me these E-mails it's
the fact that you are A very nice person in general. Once
again though thank you for the E-mail on the Irish
Bracelet. Take good care of yourself. Goodbye for now.

Your friend Alex


*Here Alex assumes Jennifer visits people she doesn't
know.*

Dear Jennifer Gilpin

I sure am glad that you had a good weekend other
than the shots that you had at the doctor. I think those
are okay although they have stung me a little bit when
the doctor puts that needle or whatever it's called in my
arm but when you have to get a shot you have to get
one. I don't think that's an optional thing.

You said that you are going to a friend's house to
watch the ice skaters at the Olympics. What's this
friend's name? Do you know? I hope you have a good
time at this friend's house tonight. Please tell me all
about it when you reply to this E-mail. I miss you very
much and hope to hear from you soon. Take good care of
yourself. Goodbye.

Love Alex Gilpin

### Alex—the spelling perfectionist?

Dear Mom

Just so you know on the E-mail where you were telling me about work you spelled dear wrong when wrote dear Alex. When you spelled dear you left out the A.

Love Alex


### Alex, who made who late?

Dear Aunt Carole

Saturday Scott and I were supposed to go to this softball tournament but we ended up not doing that because of all of these mistakes that Scott made (I mean things like waiting for me to get out of bed and taking a late shower and things like that).

Then on Monday night Scott and I went to our Social Skills group. This group is actually split up into two groups. Scott's group went out to dinner at a restaurant called Lucy's. My group stayed at the TEACCH office and played a board game called Pictionary. Our group was split into to different groups for this game and to play this game you have to watch someone draw something and you have to guess what that something is. If you get the correct answer your team gets 1 point. And whichever team has the most points at the end of the game wins. And guess what my team won. I thought that was a good night. I hope to hear from you soon. Take good care of yourself . Goodbye.

Love Alex

*Alex, no need to hope...*

Dear Dad

　　I just want to wish you A Happy Birhtday. I hope you will do something on your birthday (meaning something like going out to dinner). I really love you. I hope that you love me too. Goodbye for now.

Love Alex